Contents

Any words appearing in the text in bold, **like this**, are explained in the glossary.

Who is Queen Elizabeth II?

Elizabeth II (you say, 'the Second') is Queen of the **United Kingdom**. She is also head of a group of countries called the **Commonwealth**. Here she is with some Commonwealth leaders.

Queen Elizabeth II

Vic Parker

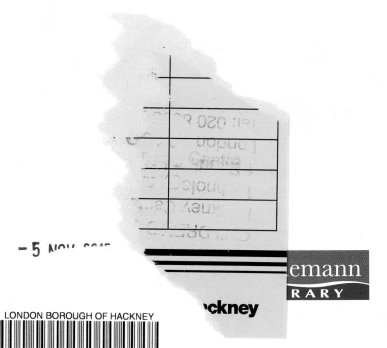

emann
RARY

www.heinemann.co.uk/library
Visit our website to find out more information about Heinemann Library books.

To order:

Phone 44 (0) 1865 888066

Send a fax to 44 (0) 1865 314091

Visit the Heinemann Bookshop at www.heinemann.co.uk/library to browse our catalogue and order online.

First published in Great Britain by Heinemann Library, Halley Court, Jordan Hill, Oxford OX2 8EJ, a division of Reed Educational and Professional Publishing Ltd.
Heinemann is a registered trademark of Reed Educational and Professional Publishing Ltd.

OXFORD MELBOURNE AUCKLAND
JOHANNESBURG BLANTYRE GABORONE
IBADAN PORTSMOUTH (NH) USA CHICAGO

Designed by Celia Floyd
Illustrated by Jeff Edwards
Originated by Dot Gradation
Printed in Hong Kong

ISBN 0 431 02460 X (hardback)
06 05 04 03 02
10 9 8 7 6 5 4 3 2 1

ISBN 0 431 02461 8 (paperback)
06 05 04 03 02
10 9 8 7 6 5 4 3 2 1

British Library Cataloguing in Publication Data

Parker, Victoris
  Queen Elizabeth II
  1.Elizabeth, II, Queen of Great Britain 2.Queens - Great Britain -
  Biography - Juvenile literature 3.Great Britain -
  History - Elizabeth II, 1952- - Juvenile literature
  I.Title
  941'.085'092

Acknowledgements
The publishers would like to thank the following for permission to reproduce photographs: Associated Press: p. 4; Camera Press: pp. 20, 22, 25, 26; Hulton Archive: pp. 8, 9, 10, 11; JS Library International: pp. 6, 18, 19, 23; John Frost Newspapers: p. 17; Popperfoto: pp. 7, 12, 13, 14, 15, 16; Rex Features: pp. 21, 24.Cover photograph reproduced with permission of Camera Press.

Every effort has been made to contact copyright holders of any material reproduced in this book. Any omissions will be rectified in subsequent printings if notice is given to the publishers.

Disclaimer
All the Internet addresses (URLs) given in this book were valid at the time of going to press. However, due to the dynamic nature of the Internet, some addresses may have changed, or sites may have ceased to exist since publication. While the author and publishers regret any inconvenience this may cause readers, no responsibility for any such changes can be accepted by either the author or the publishers.

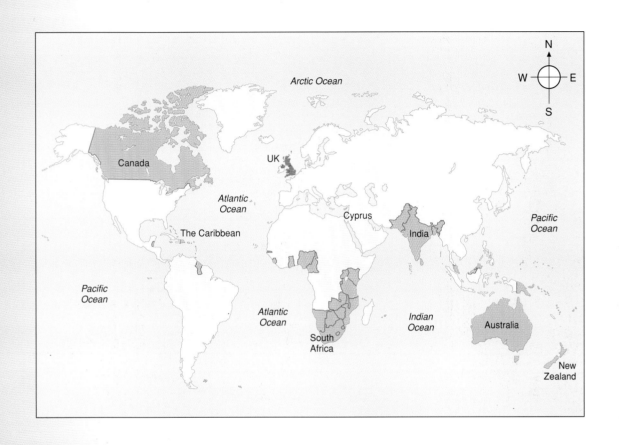

This is a map of the world. The Commonwealth countries are coloured in orange. The United Kingdom is part of the Commonwealth. We call it 'the **UK**' for short. It is red on this map.

Early years

Elizabeth was born on 21 April 1926. Her grandparents were King and Queen of the **UK**. Her parents were a **duke** and **duchess**. Elizabeth was a princess. Here is the **royal** family at baby Elizabeth's **christening**.

When Elizabeth was four years old, her parents had another baby, Margaret. Elizabeth liked looking after her little sister. They all lived in London near the King's home, Buckingham Palace.

Elizabeth at home

Elizabeth and Margaret had a **governess** called Miss Crawford. They called her Crawfie. The princesses did not go to school. Crawfie gave them lessons at home. She also played with them and put them to bed.

Elizabeth was very tidy. For her sixth birthday, she was given a playhouse. It was meant to look like a Welsh cottage. She and Margaret loved cleaning and polishing everything inside.

Elizabeth playing

Elizabeth always loved horses. She got her first pony when she was just three years old. By the time she was ten, she could ride really well.

Elizabeth enjoyed playing outdoors. At weekends her family went walking and cycling in the countryside. They went on holiday to Scotland, where the princesses went swimming at the seaside.

Moving house

When Elizabeth was ten, her father became King. People came to clap and cheer. Elizabeth smiled and waved at the crowds. Later, she wrote a story about the wonderful day.

Elizabeth and her family went to live at Buckingham Palace. Elizabeth did not like it because it was big and cold. When she was 11, she joined the Girl Guides. She enjoyed being a Guide.

Elizabeth (on the right) with other Girl Guides.

The Second World War

When Elizabeth was 13, a war broke out. Many people were killed and no one had enough food. Elizabeth wanted to cheer everyone up. She spoke on the radio to children across the world.

The war was called the Second World War. The Army needed young people to help with the war work. When Elizabeth was 19, she joined the Army. She learned to fix cars and drive trucks.

A wedding and a funeral

Elizabeth fell in love with a Navy officer called Prince Philip Mountbatten. They got married in 1947. Their son Charles was born a year later, and their daughter Anne was born in 1950.

Elizabeth and Philip were on holiday in Africa when something very sad happened. Elizabeth's father, the King, suddenly died. This meant that Elizabeth was Queen. She flew back to England at once.

Elizabeth is crowned

At her **coronation** in 1953, Elizabeth wore rich robes and sparkling jewels. People all over the world watched on television. This was the first time so many people had seen such an amazing event.

Elizabeth's husband did not change his **title**. He stayed a prince. Their son Andrew was born in 1960, and their son Edward was born four years after that.

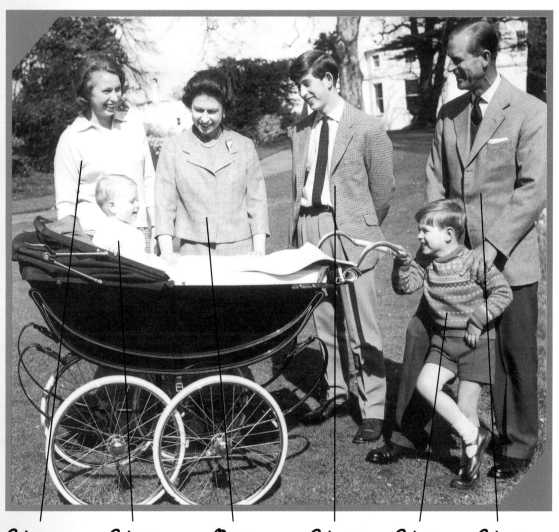

Princess Anne   Prince Edward   Queen Elizabeth   Prince Charles   Prince Andrew   Prince Philip

The Queen's work

The Queen works hard. She often talks about **government** with the **Prime Minister**. She also goes to events like the Remembrance Sunday **ceremony,** which is to remember people who died in wars. This picture shows her in the parade called **Trooping the Colour**.

Every year, the Queen goes on television to wish everybody Happy Christmas. She sends a birthday card to people who are 100 years old. She also holds ceremonies to **honour** people who have done good work.

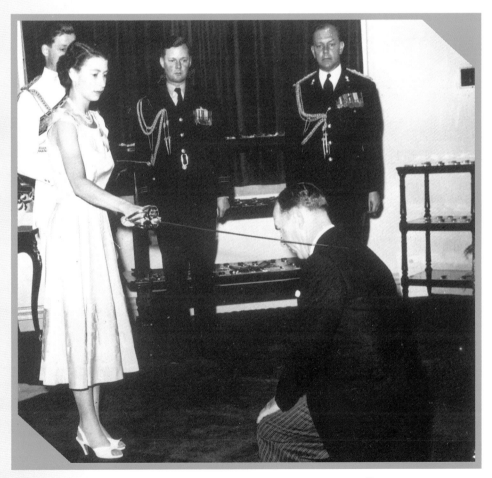

Queen Elizabeth knighting a man in Buckingham Palace.

Meeting people

The Queen often visits towns and villages in the **UK**. Lots of people wait to see her. She walks about talking to them. Every summer, she holds garden parties for hundreds of her **subjects**.

The Queen travels all over the world to meet leaders of other countries. Sometimes she invites them to Buckingham Palace. She thinks it is important that people everywhere should be friends.

Happy and sad times

The year 1977 was called Elizabeth's Silver **Jubilee**, because she had been Queen for 25 years. People were happy for her and held parties all over the **UK** and **Commonwealth**.

In 1981, a man shot at the Queen during **Trooping the Colour**. Luckily, she was not hurt. In 1992, there was a fire at her favourite home, Windsor Castle. Many of the things she loved got burned.

The Golden Jubilee

When Elizabeth first became Queen, there were no motorways, supermarkets or computers. There have been many changes in the world since then. Now people talk on mobile phones, go shopping on the Internet, and send emails.

The year 2002 is the Queen's Golden Jubilee. This means that Elizabeth has been Queen for 50 years. Events like this are celebrated all over the world. They are also special for the **royal** family.

You can find a list of the people in this photo on page 29 of this book.

Family tree

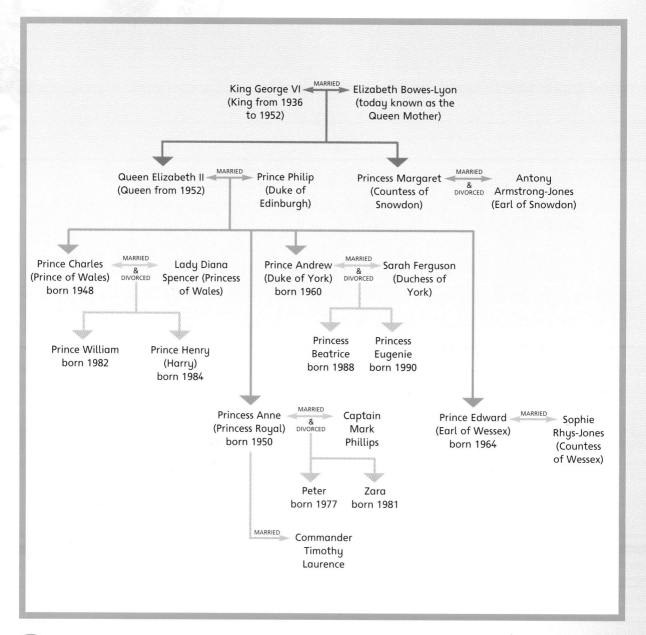

King George VI (King from 1936 to 1952) —MARRIED— Elizabeth Bowes-Lyon (today known as the Queen Mother)

Queen Elizabeth II (Queen from 1952) —MARRIED— Prince Philip (Duke of Edinburgh)

Princess Margaret (Countess of Snowdon) —MARRIED & DIVORCED— Antony Armstrong-Jones (Earl of Snowdon)

Prince Charles (Prince of Wales) born 1948 —MARRIED & DIVORCED— Lady Diana Spencer (Princess of Wales)

Prince Andrew (Duke of York) born 1960 —MARRIED & DIVORCED— Sarah Ferguson (Duchess of York)

Prince William born 1982

Prince Henry (Harry) born 1984

Princess Beatrice born 1988

Princess Eugenie born 1990

Princess Anne (Princess Royal) born 1950 —MARRIED & DIVORCED— Captain Mark Phillips

Prince Edward (Earl of Wessex) born 1964 —MARRIED— Sophie Rhys-Jones (Countess of Wessex)

Peter born 1977

Zara born 1981

Princess Anne —MARRIED— Commander Timothy Laurence

Fact file

- The Queen's full name is Elizabeth Alexandra Mary Windsor. Her nickname is Lilibet.
- The Queen's real birthday is on 21 April, when she celebrates at home with her family. She has an **official** birthday in June, when public celebrations take place.
- The Queen owns several homes in the **UK**. The most important ones are Buckingham Palace, Windsor Castle, Sandringham House and Balmoral Castle.
- The Queen receives between 200 and 300 letters every day.
- When the Queen travels abroad, she takes four and a half tons of luggage. That is even heavier than an elephant!
- You can see the Queen's picture on money and stamps in **Commonwealth** countries all over the world.
- The Queen has owned dogs called corgis since she was eighteen.
- The Queen does not choose the **Prime Minister** or other people in **government**.
- Whenever the Queen attends an important event, people there sing a song called 'God Save the Queen'.

Photograph on p. 27 (left to right): *front* – Princess Beatrice, the Queen Mother, Queen Elizabeth II, Princess Eugenie; *second row* – Prince Philip, Prince Charles, Zara Phillips, Peter Phillips, Princess Anne, Prince Andrew; *back* – Prince Harry, Prince William, two unidentified people, Commander Timothy Laurence.

Find out more

More books to read

The Coronation of Queen Elizabeth II by G. Clements (Franklin Watts)
Queen Elizabeth II by Sara Barton-Wood (Hodder Wayland)
The Royal Family by Cherry Gilchrist (Longman)
A Visit to the United Kingdom by Rachael Bell (Heinemann Library)

Places to visit

- *Balmoral Castle, Scotland* You can visit an exhibition and you can also go pony-trekking, just like the Queen does.
- *Buckingham Palace, London* You can watch the **changing of the guard** outside. In the summer, you can buy tickets to go inside.
- *Sandringham House, Norfolk* The park here is open all year.
- *The Tower of London* The **crown jewels** are on show in this big castle on the River Thames.
- *Westminster Abbey, London* The Queen was crowned and married in this cathedral (big church).
- *Windsor Castle, Berkshire* There is a dolls' house here which belonged to the Queen's grandmother when she was young.

Websites

www.royal.gov.uk The official website for the Queen and the **royal family**
www.thecommonwealth.org Click on 'Young Commonwealth' to find out about the countries in the **Commonwealth**.
www.royalyachtbritannia.co.uk The **royal** family used to have their own sailing ship, called the *Britannia*. This website will tell you all about it.

Glossary

ceremony special words and actions used at important events

changing of the guard when one group of soldiers guarding Buckingham Palace leaves and another group takes their place

christening ceremony when a new baby is taken to church to give it a name and welcome it into the Christian religion

Commonwealth a group made up of countries that were all once ruled by Britain

coronation ceremony when a person is made Queen or King

duchess/duke member of the royal family, next in importance after princess/prince

governess woman who is paid to look after children in their home and to be their teacher

government making decisions and laws for a country. The group of people who do this is also called the government.

honour let someone use a special title

Jubilee year when there is a special 'birthday' of something that happened

knighting touching a man's shoulders with a sword to honour him with the title 'Sir'

official part of a person's work, and not part of their home life

Prime Minister leader of the government

royal anything to do with a Queen, King or their family

subjects people ruled by a Queen or King

title word used before a name, like Mr, Mrs, Queen, Prince, Duchess

Trooping the Colour a parade held to celebrate the Queen's Official Birthday. It means 'marching with the flag'.

United Kingdom (UK) The country made up of England, Scotland, Wales and Northern Ireland

Index